The Art of Woodworking

A Total Beginners Guide

CONTENTS

Introduction
Chapter One: Tools and Materials
Chapter Two: Basic Techniques
Chapter Three: Beginner Projects
Chapter Four: How to Use Wood Finishers
Chapter Five: Dumbest Woodworking Mistakes
Conclusion

Introduction

For over 12,000 years, humans have been strengthening their relationship with the art and craft of woodworking. Historical findings trace the existence of wooden hunting gear back to the Neolithic era. The two oldest civilizations that discovered and exploited the true potential of woodworking were the ancient Egyptian and Chinese civilizations. Drawings of carved wooden figures that resemble stools, chairs, boats, and even houses can be found in many ancient Egyptian paintings.

Woodworking refers to the skill, ability, or even art of creating usable items or artistic figures out of wood. It's preserved its noble status for centuries as the evolution of civilization helped push woodworking forward through the use of the latest technologies and tools. While the classic chisel used in woodcarving is still largely used today, modern tools have helped broaden the range of products and applications of wood.

As you progress through this book, you'll start piecing together a deeper understanding of the type of tools and materials used to create various wooden items, in addition to the pros and cons of different techniques and equipment.

Many woodworkers find nobility in shaping a piece of life which used to be a tree into something else, while still retaining its original soul. The variations between the different types of wood in terms of physical and chemical properties only depend on the kind of tree it's cut from, but also its age and state.

There is no denying that the learning curve of woodworking can prove more difficult than many other skills. In fact, not only does it require an active imagination that allows picturing the final form of wood, but also being good with one's hands for the delicate, technical aspects of woodworking. Fortunately, you don't have to be born with innate woodworking skills to create wooden masterpieces and enjoy this century-old trade, as you'll find out in the following pages.

Chapter One: Tools and Materials

Woodworking is a vast field with infinite possibilities for conceptualization. It's common to find yourself overwhelmed by the sheer volume of solutions, tools, techniques, and artistic perspectives upon starting out. As a beginner, your first instinct should be choosing which tools and materials you'll be working with. To do so, you'll want to make sure that you're familiar with the uses of various tools and materials. If you focus too much on the final image of the wood product you want to create, you may overwhelm yourself as you attempt to select the most suitable tools for the job. As such, the first step will be to understand how wood varieties differ according to their usage and origin.

The Three Main Wood Types

As a woodworking enthusiast, you'll be choosing from three main types of wood, each with its own spectrum of properties.

- **Softwoods**

Softwood is a type of lumber obtained from a specific species of trees scientifically known as Gymnosperms, commonly referred to as conifer trees. Essentially, softwood is obtained from trees characterized by needles and cones. There are a few popular choices that woodworkers prefer to work with when it comes to woodworking and construction jobs, such as pine, Douglas fir, spruce, and redwood.

- **Hardwoods**

Unlike softwoods, hardwood trees do not produce any needles or cones. The scientific name of hardwood trees is Angiosperms, and they're the ones that commonly produce leaves and seeds. Woodworkers prefer to use oak, mahogany, walnut, and maple trees due to their unique characteristics. Some common trees known as deciduous trees, like palm and bamboo, are also used as hardwood even though they may not share all of the characteristics of previously mentioned hardwood trees. Some even refer to them as 'engineered' woods.

- **Manufactured/Engineered Wood**

The two previous types of woods occur naturally without the need for any human intervention. In contrast, engineered wood is synthetic or half-synthetic, which means that the only means to produce it is through manufacturing. Natural wood is manipulated to achieve optimal characteristics or qualities that improve its performance and utility in the woodworking process. Composite wood is a commonly used type of engineered wood, made from sawmill waste. Plywood, oriented strand board, fiber-board, and composite board are all engineered woods, made available through industrial heat and chemical treatments.

Now, it's important to understand that these three main types of woods comprise thousands of sub-species and varieties, with a myriad of properties and characteristics. While almost all types of woods are used in different applications, there are a number of popular wood varieties specially used in the art of woodworking.

Alder Wood

The natural beauty of alder wood is carving its way up the ranks of woodworking thanks to its unique flexibility and workability. The main locations where alder lumber is obtained from are North California and Southwestern Canada. It's usually compared to birch trees, seeing as they are used interchangeably in similar applications.

A freshly cut piece of alder lumber has a natural off-white color, but it's a rare color to see because the tint can change quickly when the lumber is exposed to sunlight and air. As a woodworker, this type of medium-density wood is employed in carving, turning, and machining applications due to its straight grain. Finishing treatments shouldn't pose any issues due to the smooth surface that can be easily stained or painted after sanding. Woodworkers who are interested in working on bigger solid or one-body wood pieces tend to avoid alder wood because the height of the tree isn't very impressive. Obtaining larger pieces can cost extra as they are considered quite rare. You'll find alder wood to be a popular variety for cabinets, furniture, and decorative pieces like carvings and frames. Another special characteristic of Alder wood is its clean musical tone, making it one of the most favored types of wood when it comes to shaping electric guitars. Even more expensive varieties like mahogany do not match the pristine tone of alder wood.

Ash Wood

Ash wood used to be a common variety of wood until a recent pest started invading the trees, causing them to die prematurely. Ash is a more budget-friendly version of oak wood that shares the majority of its special characteristics. The staining process is also beginner-friendly, and it can be utilized cleverly in a myriad of projects and applications. It's quite abundant and affordable in Europe, parts of Asia, and North America.

Aspen

The fuzzy texture of aspen wood is one of its most defining characteristics, in addition to being a lightweight hardwood. It has natural light colors that can handle painting or staining with relative ease. The main aspen regions are in Northeast America, but they are not easily available all the time, making them centralized around certain projects that specifically require aspen wood. The most popular usage of aspen is in the building of saunas thanks to its extremely limited heat conduction and moisture absorption.

Aspen wood is also used in making matchsticks due to its low conductivity, as well as the building of certain furniture pieces. They're particularly desirable in building drawers because they limit the risk of sticking to other furniture pieces. Its rare odorless and tasteless properties make it an ideal material for the manufacturing of cooking utensils.

Balsa

Balsa is considered one of the lightest variations of hardwood as far as weight. It's used by hobbyist woodworkers in creative and craft-specific types of projects. Its main weakness is its relatively low strength, making it not the most suitable wood type for practical-oriented and classical woodworkers. While it may not be popular with expert woodworkers, it's one of the best varieties that can be used by beginners and enthusiasts. Balsa's lightness means that it has high buoyancy, making it a very common type of wood for building small rafts and life preservers. Surfboards are another artistic and practical use of balsa wood, which explains why Balsa is so popular among artistically-inclined woodworkers.

Bamboo

Although bamboo is technically a strand of grass, it's also considered a hardwood due to its shared similarities with other types of hardwood. It's easily found in tropical climates, with species varying according to the region. The veneer product of bamboo, used in engineered varieties like plywood, is obtained by cutting the bamboo stem very thinly.

Many mistake bamboo to be softer than most woods, yet it's actually a very tough type that can be compared to red oak and maple in terms of hardness. The colorful green gradients of bamboo make it a stylistic type of wood that's used in garden decorations and furniture; some even use it for flooring thanks to its elasticity and sturdiness.

American Oak

The crown of the American oak is wide and dome-shaped. The tree has a short, straight trunk; the branches form wreaths. The shiny reddish brown twigs are bare and warty and dull shiny and grayish in later life. The pointed buds are dark red to brownish.
The bark is smooth and silver-gray. Rotation can easily occur if the bark is damaged. Under normal circumstances the trunk becomes 24-36" thick, although exceptions of 60" thickness are known.
The wood of the American oak is less durable and has a coarser structure than the wood of the summer oak (Quercus robur). The hard and tough heartwood has a red-brown color. The wood is used for floors and furniture.

Other wood types

There are of course many other types of wood and each of them has specific properties. Below you will find an image with different types of wood and their specific wood grain.

Psychological and Personal Attributes of a Woodworker

Regardless of the type of wood and the tools used in a woodworking project, the sharpest tool in your shed should be you. As an aspiring woodworker, there are a number of skills and masteries that you should have in your arsenal.
- **Technical Knowledge**

Whether you want to become a carpenter or a creative designer, you need to have a firm grasp on various concepts like finishing, framing, and utilization of tools. You don't need to attend a specific woodworking program to get a certificate, but you'll want to make sure that you get some form of training from skilled experts in the field.
- **Patience**

Just like doing anything worthwhile, beginnings can be slow. Don't expect to master a new craft without spending hours and hours practicing and training. Your dedication to woodworking should inspire you to keep going forward, even if you're not entirely satisfied with the current results.

- **Creativity**

While creativity isn't something that you can just learn from a book, it can still be a direction that you can choose. Try to think outside the box if you're interested in woodworking, beyond the conventional carpenter path. Check out the works of other craftsmen and artists to peek into their thinking process. Creativity can also be employed in practical-oriented woodworking projects.

- **Numerical Knowledge**

While some woodworkers despise mathematics, it remains an essential component in almost all woodworking projects. As such, you'll want to familiarize yourself with basic and elemental calculations, in addition to learning how to read blueprints to know how to put together and preview a project.

Indispensable Woodworking Tools

For anyone to be able to work with wood, they need tools. Some essential tools exist in almost any handiwork project, like hammers and nails, but there are also specific woodworking tools that you should have in your toolset before you can begin any project. You don't want to abruptly stop halfway simply because you're missing the right tool, or compromise and use an unsuitable tool that will produce poor results.

- **Workbench**

For starters you'll need a place to work. You can easily find a portable one with vise included. Alternatively a standard work surface is also sufficient but adding a vise is recommended.

- **Clamps**

When sawing pieces of wood you need to clamp the wood to your workbench. This will ensure that your cut is straight and will prevent the wood of cracking and deforming when finishing your cut. Two pieces will be sufficient for most of your projects.

- **(Cordless) Electrical screwdriver**

This will be your main work tool for woodworking. The cordless type is extremely handy but be sure to have a spare battery. Complement your screwdriver with a variety of bits. For small holes there are universal bits while for larger ones you can find lip and spur bits or for even larger holes wood spade types. Additionally you'll need also a set of at least Philips and slot drill bits.

- **Handsaw and mitre box**

These come as well in a variety. Investing in one 15" handsaw and one mitre saw. Additionally you should find yourself a mitre box as well as these are essential in cutting straight and angled edges.

- **Framing square**

When the pieces are too large for in your mitre box you'll need an L framing square. Size 8" to 12" is a good place to start. Make sure the front and backside has a measurable design.

- **Claw Hammer**

No matter the nature of the project you're undertaking, a claw hammer is always an indispensable tool. It's a very common household tool that has a claw-looking head, which allows it to extract nails from wood planks or walls. The claw head is on one side of the metallic body of the hammer, counterbalanced by a flat side that can be used to hammer down objects. Be careful not to use waffle-head hammers, the other popular type of hammer, since hammering wood with them will leave displeasing marks.

- **Stud finder**

A Studfinder is a device used to locate framing studs in wood buildings which are usually located behind a drywall. These devices are handheld and come in two categories: magnetic and electric.

- **Measuring Tape**

Given that wood is (almost always) cut to fit the physical description of the final product, you need to have a measuring tape with you at all times. You can also use the tape to find the most accurate center point on a wooden board. It's advisable to get a retractable version that is at least 25 feet long. The hook end of the measuring tape should always be firm to ensure that you get accurate readings.

- **Moisture Meter**

Any long-term woodworking project requires a moisture meter to be properly carried out. You shouldn't use lumber of unknown moisture percentage, especially if you're using different types of lumber in your project. Moisture meters can have small pins that can penetrate the wood to a certain depth, and scan for the actual percentage of moisture. Some pin-less meters are often used to avoid leaving a dent or mark in the wood. The best moisture meter for you should have different reading capabilities to analyze different types of wood.

- **Chisel and Screwdriver**

Chisels can vary in size and uses according to the variety of wood and kind of project. As a woodworker, you'll be using the chisel to clean out dents in joints and saw cuts. The preferred material for most woodworkers is carbon steel. Make sure to get equipped with an assortment of chisels that cover various sizes.

Similar to chisels, screwdrivers come in sizes, materials, and shapes. You may be familiar with the popular ones used in construction, such as Philips and slot, but you'll also need other types in your set; look for star drivers and Torx drivers as well. Make sure you get a variety of thin, thick, light, and heavy screwdrivers to accommodate the needs of your future projects.

- **Level**

For bigger projects a level will be essential. This tool will make sure your planes are nice and straight even if you're working horizontally or vertically. A liquid type is perfectly fine to begin with.

- **Sandpaper**

You will always need to sand your project down once you're finished or sometimes even during your project. Sandpapers come in different grits. The grit number defines the coarseness of the sandpaper. Having a fine, medium and coarse type is sufficient for most uses. Look for grit ranging from 50 to 300.

- **Pencil**

You'll need pencils to make markings onto the wood. Make sure to take one with a big tip. A standard drawing pencil will break too easily.

- **Brushes**

To apply a wood finisher you'll need a couple of brushes. These can be standard paint brushes. Buy the correct size based on the size of your project.

Taking Care and Maintaining Woodworking Tools

After investing a lot of money in your tools, the last thing you want to do is leave them without maintenance. Maintaining your tools directly impacts the success of your projects. Ill-maintained or ragged tools can ruin many details in your design. There are some proper techniques used by expert woodworkers that you can use to keep your equipment in tip-top shape.

Make sure all your blade-type tools remain as sharp as new. You can use manual or automatic sharpening tools, depending on your needs. Your sawblades are the most important blade-type tools you need to keep an eye on constantly, because they degrade easily from the constant cutting and suffer from wear and tear.

Wood Finishers

Commonly referred to as furniture finishers, wood finishers are used in a great number of woodworking projects. They're used to remove moisture and enrich the color of the wood. Several types of finishers revolve around painting, coating, or staining wood to highlight certain aesthetic aspects or safety features and designs. The most common types of finishers are surface finishing and penetrating finishing. The former is often used by woodworkers who want to keep the product as clean and natural-looking as possible; it's also quite easier to apply because this is done on the surface.

On the other hand, penetrating finishing is a more invasive finishing because it takes place inside the furniture or wood product itself. It's more durable than surface finishing, yet it lacks the clean and natural look provided by surface finishing. Some woodworkers add linseed, Danish, and Tung oils to embolden the colors of the wood.

Chapter Two: Basic Techniques

Many people are under the impression that wood workmanship requires pricey tools to be able to do the job correctly. This couldn't be further away from the truth. While expensive tools might indeed make your job easier, they don't necessarily make it better. Just like prepping lumber, if you have a table saw and a thirteen-inch-thick planer, then it will be a straightforward project for you. However, if you prefer using hand tools to have more control over your work, you will need to put in extra effort to learn these techniques. In the past, artisans worked with their lumber using only hand tools before machines took over the furniture industry.

You will be amazed at how woodworking by hand can be more viable and efficient in executing masterpieces. There are many tested and proven techniques that we can become competent in to free us from the necessity of using machines or buying expensive tools. These basic techniques require some effort and a bit of research to master.

Understanding the Behavior of Wood

It's never a clever idea to begin using your tools at random without understanding how wood behaves and the right direction for planing your wood. This means that if you want to make horizontal, vertical, or inclined flat surfaces on your workpiece, you will need enough knowledge of how wood behaves. When trees grow, there are layers of growth rings that start to form. These grains can be shown beautifully in the boards we cut; that said, these grains can be a major obstacle for people who don't understand the ideal direction of planing.

Other than the direction of cutting, you'll also need to learn more about how wood expands and contracts during the different fluctuations of humidity throughout the seasons. This is why every woodworker takes into consideration these natural properties before approaching any project, to avoid disastrous and wasteful results.

The Importance of Sharpening

There is a common misconception that woodwork is extremely hard. People have perpetuated this myth long enough, and this is mainly because they were using dull tools all along. It's accepted among woodworkers to "Let the tool do the work". If the tool you're using requires a lot of effort to do its job, whether it's cutting, shaping, or manipulating your workpiece in any way, then you're probably using a dull tool. This is why sharpening your tools is a fundamental skill that every woodworker needs to acquire and integrate into their work routine. Working with unsharpened tools doesn't only waste time and effort that you could have saved, but it can also prove very dangerous. Applying your bodyweight on cutting a piece of wood with a dull tool might lead to hazardous situations; when the tool finally breaks free, you will lose control, and it will stab into whichever body part is in its path. As such, it's essential that you understand the power and need of sharpening your tools, and how to do it in order to prevent risks and waste valuable effort.

Making a Straight Cut

All you need for this technique is a pencil, a piece of wood, and a saw blade. Firstly, start by drawing a straight line using a pencil on the piece of wood you are cutting. Alternatively, you can print out cutting lines of your project and fix them with packing tape. Next, line up the saw blade correctly with the edge of your piece of lumber, right where you drew the line. To realize your straight cut, bear in mind that saws don't actually cut perfectly straight lines. They tend to veer slightly to the right. This means that you have to angle your workpiece slightly to achieve a straight cut. Lastly, make sure that you adjust your saw while cutting to the angle you are holding the wood. Don't forget to hold your workpiece firmly to prevent it from shifting or bouncing around on the saw deck.

Perfecting a Curved Cut

Curved cuts, on the other hand, only require the saw blade to be lined with the edge of the wood where you'll start your cut. Just like straight cuts, you'll still need to use a pencil. This time, draw a curved, wavy line just like the cut you want on the piece of wood you're working on. Gentle curves are always much easier than tight ones. The following thing you need to do is to start cutting your workpiece, but at a slight angle towards the top of your first curve. After placing your lumber, switch your saw on and start cutting the wood without forcing the piece against the saw blade. Instead, apply gentle pressure to ensure that your lumber is feeding through the saw. Make sure to keep turning your lumber smoothly and continuously in a movement that mimics the curved line you drew. This process requires dexterity and patience. It's best to practice simple curves before moving on to more complex and tight curved lines.

Hand-Cut Miter

The process of cutting miters can quickly go south without proper knowledge and practice. While the process is fairly easy with a proper miter saw or a chop saw, these expensive tools can be replaced with hand tools when you learn how to manage miter joints perfectly. To explain this technique, we'll use the example of a 45-degree miter seeing as it's the most commonly used type.
Start by marking your 45-degree lines, and then join them by a 90-degree one. The first lines are for knowing where to cut, while the other serves as a guide to achieve straight cuts between the 45-degree angled ones. Make sure that you're cutting slowly and parallel to the 90-degree line. With enough practice, you'll be able to reach the level of precision required to make perfect 45-degree cuts.

Hand Planes

Most working tools are pretty self-explanatory, yet not all of them can be handled by intuition. For example, the use of hand planes can go wrong without proper understanding of this basic technique. In fact, the edge might become askew, or you might face a problem with the cap iron to place it correctly. Learning to use hand planes requires some time and effort to understand the instructions and practice how to cut from coarse-to-fine. While this might seem hard for beginners, with a bit of specialized research, you'll come to realize that properly tuning up hand planes is a simple and easily attainable skill.
Since woodworking requires working with your hands to acquire and perfect its skills, you'll inevitably need to practice any skill you learn. To do so, all you need is an old plane, after which you can hop on YouTube and start following every step in how-to instructional videos.

Cutting Dovetails and Mortise and Tenon Joints

For making boxes, using the dovetail joint is the most preferred and effective technique to join board corners together. You'll need to cut tails, trace them on the board, and then cut out the waste you traced.
A mortise joint is one of the most fundamental techniques in woodworking. They are the perfect "fit" for joining any horizontal and vertical pieces by interlocking both pieces at a 90-degree angle. For example, fitting chair rails and legs is done best by fitting a tenon into the mortise. With regular practice, you'll improve your ability to achieve tight fits effortlessly. However, it's imperative to first learn about the different ways you can make a mortise, along with choosing the right width of the tenon you'll be using. Cutting a tenon is achieved with a few straight cuts, just as previously explained.

Sanding Your Project

Cutting and drilling holes will result in splinters and burs on the surface of the wood. To complete your project, you'll need to sand it and smoothen it in order to get rid of these imperfections. There are different types of sanders, from basic sandpaper to more complicated sanding equipment. Here are some main types of sanding along with their working method.

- *Hand Sanders:* These are the simplest tools and the perfect choice for beginners to smoothen out wood projects. They come with a plate and a handle that you can be placed at the bottom of the sander to use. While they are certainly cheaper and easier, their only downside is that they require a good deal of patience and time to achieve the perfect finish.
- *Orbital Sanders:* This type is perfect for tight and small places. These sanders require sanding desks for optimal control.
- *Belt Sanders:* These are the most effective and heavy-duty sanders. They're more suitable for large flat-surfaced workpieces as they can work quickly and effectively through a lot of material.

Since making your workpiece smoother requires the right grit of sandpaper, it's better for beginners to be on the safe side and go for a medium grit given its suitability for most projects. Start sanding your project in long, straight motions while paying attention to edges and corners. Make sure to sand along the natural grain of the wood to avoid leaving any damaging marks across. You can then choose a finer grit of sanding paper for more satisfying results until you achieve the smoothness you want for your project.

Finishing Your Piece

Teaching yourself how to manipulate wood and the use of different machines and tools to bring your vision to life is an incredibly enriching and rewarding activity. That said, your project won't be complete until you finish the wood.

After spending hours and efforts into your art piece, it'd be unfair to leave it unfinished. Generally, rubbing the piece with oil isn't considered a proper finishing technique for your workpiece after all the backbreaking work that went into it. Proper finishes won't only beautify your project, but they'll also protect it and ensure its longevity.

There are many finishing techniques that you can choose. Among them, shellac is perhaps the most common method to finish wood pieces flawlessly. Once you get the hang of applying these techniques, you'll find that they are quick, easy, very forgiving, and repairable for the most part. Since the brush is dipped in alcohol, you won't even have to clean your brush as it will re-soften. Also, you have plenty of varnish options to protect your project for outdoor use.

Woodworking isn't just a matter of being handy. Through the use of different techniques, you are allowing yourself to get connected with a long history of craftsmanship. Since this is one of the earliest skills mankind developed, techniques have evolved to allow for shaping and manipulating wood in ever more advanced and sophisticated ways. Ultimately, to reach this level of proficiency, you'll need to begin by knowing and understanding these basic techniques before you can start developing your own style.

Chapter Three: Beginner Projects

It's always best to start small and then work your way up with your woodworking projects. Never think of something minor as a waste of time. You're already honing your craft, and you need all the practice that you can get. So, start by familiarizing yourself with all your tools, machines, your workbench, and then get to work. All you need are your materials, patience, determination, and some elbow grease to craft some superb handmade projects. It could also be helpful to take notes about your impressions for every step, detailing which parts were easy and which were difficult. But let's dive right in and check out some compelling beginner projects that you can start with.

Shoe Organizer

You can enjoy building a super practical shoe organizer to keep your shoes off your floor and have them neatly organized and hanging on the wall. You can rest assured that it will be solid and durable enough to hold your normal work shoes, sneakers, winter boots, sandals, and much more. Making it won't cost you more than $20-25 from start to finish. Let's list the materials and tools that you'll need for this project:
- Clamps.
- Tape measure.
- Wood glue.
- 4-in-one screwdriver.
- 5 or 8-inch dowels.
- 1-5 or 8-inch screws.
- Toggle bolts or 3-inch screws.
- 1x3 and 1x4 wood pieces.
- Miter saw.
- Drill or cordless drill.
- Countersink drill bit.

For starters, you're going to need a long wooden board – the length is up to you, depending on your number of shoe pairs and wall length. Drill three holes for your dowels, then get another scrap of wood and cut some dowel supports. Get your 1x3 piece and clamp it to a scrap piece of wood to prevent any splintering. Drill your board through the back of the 1x4 piece into your 1x3 supports. After that, you will need to glue together the screws. When cutting the 1x4 piece, remember to make it fit your shoes, which could be about 10 to 12 inches wide.

Start gluing your dowels into the support pieces. You can leave 2 or 3 inches to go beyond the support; that can be a handy way to hang your slippers or sandals. Before you can mount your shoe ladder on your wall, remember to apply a nice finish after making sure everything is perfectly smooth. Next, screw it onto your wall using your 3-inch screws or toggle bolts to hold the structure in place. When you're done, your shoe organizer will be ready for use.

Small Desk for Kids

You can build a small wall-mounted desk for your kids to play or draw on. It's a very easy project that will take you less than an hour to complete. Pick out a nice wooden board and choose which corner of the room would be best for your kids to enjoy this little desk. This could serve as a space for them to do their homework, too. It's a very clean and modern-looking design that would go well with any room. Now, let's take a closer look at the tools and materials you'll need for this project:

- Clean pieces of cloth.
- Tape measure.
- Stud finder.
- Pencil.
- Measuring level.
- Sander or electric sander.
- Power drill.
- Wood stain and conditioner.
- Sandpaper.
- 6 wood screws (5 or 8 inches).
- 6 wood screws (2 inches).
- 19.5-inch metal shelf brackets (2 brackets).
- 1 wood board (2x3 feet long, 3/4 inches thick).

Once you've got everything, use your stud finder on your wall and find two studs. Go ahead and mark them with your pencil. Use your tape measure to mark the desk height based on your children's height; most desks are typically between 23 and 27 inches, but you can make it slightly bigger (up to 30 inches) so they can grow into it. You can go for 8 to 12 inches between your child's seat and the bottom of the desk, but note that it can be more depending on how big your child is. Afterwards, bring your drill and brackets since it's time to drill and attach those to your wall using the 2-inch screws. Remember to use your measuring level to make sure it's perfectly balanced and straight.

Start using your sandpaper on your board to smoothen it out, then wipe away any dust with your cloth pieces. Next, condition the board and leave it to dry for 5 good minutes. Once that's done, start staining your wood board on both sides and let that dry for at least 2 hours. You can then attach your board to your brackets and hold your board tight when you start drilling. Drill in the 5 or 8-inch screws from the bottom to firmly attach it to the wall and brackets. When you're done, get your child's chair and belongings, be it toys or school supplies, and the desk will be fully safe and operational.

Wooden Bench

Wouldn't it be nice to have a durable and nice-looking wooden bench in your backyard or garden? It won't be difficult to make, requiring just a few hours to finish (give or take). That one is another cheap project that would probably cost you $25 to $50, which is much more affordable than buying one. So, let's have a look at the material and tools you'll need for a lovely backyard/garden bench:

- Saw or circular saw.
- Speed square.
- Driver.
- Countersink drill bit.
- Cordless drill.
- Two 1/2-inch deck screws.
- Exterior finish.
- Construction adhesive.
- 2 10-foot wood boards (2x8s).
- Wood glue.

Start cutting the angles on your wood boards and make 22.5-degree cuts. Do this 5 times to make your four bench legs. Start clamping the back and seat to your workbench, then drill and screw the front legs to the rear legs. After that, lay out and assemble the rest of the legs using the back and seat for your alignment. Then, you'll need to join the legs together – remember to use your 1/2-inch deck screws and the construction adhesive. Use your countersink drill bit to prevent the wood from splitting when you're drilling the screw holes. Also, start setting each side parallel to each other. Use glue to get your seat and the back attached firmly, then screw them into place perfectly. When you're done, coat the entire bench with the exterior finish, and leave it to dry for a few hours. Your bench should now be ready, and you can have a nice seat to relax on whenever you want.

Magazine Storage Container

We could always use a nice storage container to keep our magazines and catalogs neatly put away in one place. They can be used for filing work papers and important folders, too. It'll be a lot easier to choose between each one, and you won't get lost because they're not towering on top of each other in a messy pile. Now, let's get our materials and tools ready for these delightful containers, shall we?

- 5-gallon bucket.
- Air hose and air compressor for powering your tools.
- Circular saw.
- Drill bit set.
- Cordless drill.
- Jigsaw.
- Tape.
- 1-inch nails.
- Nail gun.
- Orbital sander.
- 2x4 ft. sheet of 1/4-inch thick plywood (2).
- 6 ft. long 1x4s pine sheet (2).

Start by marking the cuts on your wood sheets. Cut your two plywood sheets into eight pieces. Your cuts should be measured to be 11.5-in. x 11-in. pieces. Then, you'll need to trace an S-curve by using your 5-gallon bucket. Measure precisely, because the curve should be traced from the 11.5-inch high corner and across the plywood to the opposite side that's precisely at the 6-inch mark. This will give it a nice smooth curve. Now, it's time to cut each curve with your jigsaw by stacking together each wooden pair. Use your tape to stick all the sheets together to flush at each edge. Use your jigsaw on all the curves and cut them using the gang-cut technique.

Once you're done, use your saw to cut your pine sheets. The length of each cut should be 6-inch, 9.5-inch, and 11.5-inch. After that, get your cordless drill and drill 1-inch diameter finger pulls in your 6-inch pieces. Finally, you can nail all the pieces to the frames to form the containers. Sand each container well, then apply your finisher and stain. After leaving it to dry for a couple of hours, they will be ready to use and you can store all your magazines and important papers conveniently.

Double-Decker Storage Shelves

You can never run out of stuff to put on your shelves, and this double-decker shelf idea can be a great project to undertake. You can make it for your garage to store your tools and other items, or for your kitchen to arrange all your jars and spice containers up there. Some people like using these double-decker shelves in the living room to display their memorabilia or family pictures. Moreover, you could use it in your bedroom closet for extra space-saving storage. The choice is up to you and you can get as creative as you wish with your shelves. So, here's a list of what you'll need to make it the right way:

- Table saw.
- Circular saw.
- Cordless drill.
- Construction adhesive.
- Exterior finish.
- Wood stain.
- Sandpaper.
- Stud finder.
- Measurement level.
- 4-inch Lag screws and 1-5/8-inch screws.
- Plywood pieces (1x2, 1x3, 1x8, and 2x8)

For starters, keep in mind that the length of the shelf can be different depending on your space and needs. So, it could be longer or shorter, if you want.

Firstly, start cutting your plywood for the 16-inch top shelf using your circular saw and table saw. Then, you'll need to screw every frame together. Start drilling your 4-inch lag screws and 1-5/8-inch screws properly because you need them to secure the 1x8 plywood piece, which will be your back rim, and your 1x2 plywood piece, which will be your front rim. Connect them firmly to the 2x8 support block. After everything is secure, it's time to assemble your shelf fully and install your plywood bottom and top parts. Also, assemble the 1x2 and 1x3 lips properly, but remember to always use your construction adhesive to ensure that it's strong and durable. Use your measurement level to make sure everything is straight.

When you're done, start sanding every part of your shelf, then apply your exterior finish. Once you've left it to dry for 5 minutes, you can apply your wood stain, and then leave it to dry for a few hours before you can attach it to your wall. Once it's dry, use your stud finder on the wall to find the right spots for the attachment part. Remember to mark the spots and then position the double-decker shelf perfectly. Then, you can safely use your 4-inch lag screws to firmly secure the 1x8 back rim to the marked spots of the wall studs. Remember to drive two screws into each of the marked studs for better strength. Now, you can finally start using your shelf to store all your tools and items securely, or you could display your family photos to show your guests.

Building something new is always exciting, regardless of how small it is. Woodworking is an art that must be respected, and you simply can't rush art. This is indeed the perfect time to explore various techniques and learn how to build some amazing woodworking projects. It's a truly gratifying feeling when you finish building something, and then contemplate your fine handy work at the end. Eventually, you'll build enough beginner projects until you can tackle something bigger and harder, once you've gained more experience and skill.

Chapter Four: How to Use Wood Finishers

All types of wood objects and furniture need a finisher. Finishers dry to form a protective layer from moisture, stains, dirt, scratches, and other damaging elements. Wood can also expand if a finisher isn't used, which is why you might find within your home doors, cupboards, or dressers that do not shut properly. Finishers also give wood its final luster and shine.

This chapter will equip you with strong knowledge on the types of wood finishers available, how they differ from each other, how to choose the right one for your project, and how to use it.

When handling finishers, you need to be extra careful because of the chemicals in their composition. These chemicals can damage your skin when they come in direct contact with it, and may also produce fumes, some of which may be hazardous to your health.

A Few Precautions to Take

For starters, you should always be in the right gear when handling finishers. Gear includes:
- **Protective Gloves:** like a thin, surgical pair of gloves.
- **Goggles:** Protective glasses or goggles that will prevent any irritant from getting into your eyes.
- **Protective Mask:** You can wear a surgical mask or even your favorite bandana while working with a finisher.

Aside from wearing protective gear, you should always work with finishers in a well-ventilated place, preferably outdoors or in your garage. Also, make sure you never work with any flame or anything flammable near you.

Two Broad Categories of Finishers

When it comes to finishers, there are two mainly used types:
1. **Surface Finishers:** These finishers dry atop the wood. They are easy to apply, but usually don't leave a natural look on the wood. They're often used on items that go through a lot of daily wear. Varnish, for instance, is a common and widely used surface finisher.
2. **Penetrating Finishers:** As the name suggests, this type of finisher penetrates into the wood. Penetrating finishers are good for items that do not go through much wear and tear, such as antique furniture pieces.

Useful Advice on How to Use Wood Finishers

Here are some ways to give your projects a professional, clean finishing look.

Sanding: The first step in any project is to repair the wood. Depending on the type of finisher you want to use, you'll necessarily have to do some sanding to get a perfectly smooth touch. When using sandpaper, fold each paper into quarters, and further fold each quarter into thirds. Make sure you sand with the grain down to avoid scratches that might only show up after you apply stain or oil-based finishers.

Remove Dust: Always take the time to wipe away excess dust and debris resulting from the sanding process before applying any type of finisher.

Stir, Don't Shake: All finishers should be stirred before application. Don't shake a container of finisher since shaking causes air bubbles, which in turn can leave pockmarks on the surface of the wood.

Using a Brush: Finishers can be either applied with a brush, a cloth, or in spray form. Using a brush requires a different technique and can be more difficult for the absolute beginner. When using a brush, avoid dragging the brush over the edge of the can after dipping it into the finisher, because that tends to get rid of the finish before it ever reaches the wooden item. Instead, knock the brush lightly on the side of the can to remove the excess finish. Use long, straight strokes that move along the woodgrain. Use the very tip of the brush bristles when applying the finish. Continue moving in long, consistent strokes, going from one end of the piece you are working on to the other. This technique is called tipping off, which effectively reduces brush marks.

Paste Wax: Apply a finishing paste wax with a very fine steel wool pad. Make sure to always follow in the direction of the grain. After it dries, you can buff it with a clean cloth. For curves and grooves in wood that are difficult to get into, try using a shoe brush.

Wipe on Finish: Some wooden pieces will look nicer with a hand-rubbed look. This is especially true with older pieces of furniture. Here, you can consider using a wipe on finish, which is easy to apply and renders a lovely luster.

Types of Wood Finishers and How to Use Them

Let's take a more detailed look at the different wood finishers you can use.

How to Use Wood Stain (Dyes)

You can first start by using a pre-stain wood conditioner. Apply this conditioner with the tip of a brush and allow it to set for 5 to 15 minutes. Then remove any excess conditioner that isn't being absorbed by the wood. After that, you're ready to stain. Since wood stain has the effect of a dye, it changes the color of the wood, but the grain is still visible. Remember that the longer you keep the stain on, the darker the shade will get.

Once you apply the stain, remove all the excess stain as you want to let it dry on the surface of the wood, and not in the wood. Remove this excess with a cloth, moving in the direction of the grain, then leave to dry for around 4 hours. If you still prefer a darker color, repeat the same process again until you get the color you want.

Depending on your project, there are plenty of colors to choose from. However, it's important to note that the color that appears at the end depends on the variety of wood you are applying the wood stain to. To be on the safe side, use the wood stain on a separate piece of wood the same as your project. Wait for it to dry, and see if that is the shade you want. Intense colors, for instance, can be diluted with mineral spirits. Likewise, you can apply several coats if the dye is too weak.

Wood stain does enhance the look of the wood substantially, but in terms of protecting the wood, it is considered quite weak. Oftentimes, it's recommended to use a protective coat over it, like a varnish.

You can apply wood stain either with a piece of cloth or a brush. Sometimes, the application of it might slightly raise the grain, but some light sanding in between coats or using steel wool can give the wood a smoother finish.

Using Oil

Oil makes the wood look great, and is protective since it replaces the natural oils lost in the wood. Oil is one of the easiest finishers to use, given that you don't have to worry much about it after applying. If dust collects on the oiled item, you simply wipe it off. Another advantage is that oil easily hides scratches that can occur over time. All you need to do is to add oil to a clean cloth, and wipe it over the scratch.

However, oil doesn't typically provide very good protection. It doesn't change the color of the wood, but can add a yellowish tint to it or enhance the current color. For a glossier look and more protection, you would have to add paste wax on top.

There are plenty of oils to choose from. They include linseed oil, tung oil, teak oil, mineral oil, Danish oil, among many others to give your project a natural looking finish. Danish oil is perhaps the most protective of all because although oils do protect, they don't protect to the same degree than varnish does, for example. Still, Danish oil does have some varnish in it, which makes it the most protective oil.

Depending on how much protection you want for the wood, you can make your choice. For instance, a picture frame doesn't need much protection; using linseed oil is a good, inexpensive purchase. A tabletop, on the other hand, needs more protection; here Danish oil would be your best option. Other oils such as pure tung, walnut, or beeswax are food safe, so they would be good for wooden cutting boards.

Using Varnish

Varnish is made up of resin and solvents. It's great for such things as outdoor patio furniture because it offers superior UV protection. The strongest type of varnish is polyurethane. That said, this material often gives a plastic look and feel to the wood, which many people might not want depending on their personal preference. Of note, varnishes tend to dry slowly.

Using Shellac

This finisher is very user-friendly. Naturally low in fumes, shellac is usually mixed with an alcohol solvent which makes it easier to apply. It typically gives a shiny, glossy finish. Its application will most likely either be through a brush, or through an aerosol can (spray). Many people will use it on fine antiques by applying several layers of very thin coats.

Sand-waxed shellac might give a tinge of amber to the wood. There is also a choice of D wax, which is slightly more transparent. D wax shellac is used most when you are also using other topcoat products. That means you can use other products, and top off your wood surface with D wax. Another advantage is that it is very repairable, and you can easily refresh the finish of a project that uses shellac.

Using Lacquer

You probably have lacquer in every piece of wooden item in your home, since it is the most commonly used finisher in mass-produced items. The reason it's so popular h in the industry is partly because it dries extremely quickly. This means less time needed for recoating, and less chances of dust getting onto it. The commercial types are typically more industrial than other types bought off the supply store shelf, because wood manufacturers need specific features in the finishers they use.

Lacquer is a thin, liquid type of finisher. While it's usually applied by spray, this might not be the ideal method for hobbyists at home if they don't have the proper means or know-how to spray finishers. It has a lot of advantages, being durable, hard-wearing, plus it can be polished on a glossy finish. Using lacquer will give a clear and natural look to the wood after application.

Using Finishing Wax

Finishing wax is typically made from beeswax. It brings out a beautiful natural color, but not as rich and deep as oil-based finishers. You should apply it sparingly, using circular motions with a piece of clean cloth. It gives a matte finish yet can still be buffed after it dries which, giving it a smoother and glossier look.

Wax can be applied to a piece of wood once or twice a year to give it a long-lasting protective seal. Finishing wax only works best for indoor pieces, so you probably wouldn't want to use it on any outdoor wood furniture. When using finishing wax with another material, such as oil, always apply the finishing wax last.

These are the major and most commonly used types of wood finishers on the market. Each one has unique properties, and can be used differently depending on the kind project and the type of wood employed. These finishers will top off your work with a lustrous shine and protective coat for the wood.

37

Chapter Five: Dumbest Woodworking Mistakes

Woodworking requires great skill and dexterity to produce beautiful artifacts. However, a silly mistake can quickly ruin your craft, which can be costly if you're forced to throw away the damaged wood. Mistakes are no rare occurrence, but in some instances, other errors are frankly dumb and can lead to physical injuries. As such, this chapter focuses on the dumbest woodworking pitfalls mistakes that you should avoid as a beginner.

Safety First

The primary concern in woodworking is that safety comes first. You should make sure your workshop is clear of the clutter that can hinder your progress and jeopardize your safety. When operating power equipment, it's crucial to be extremely cautious to prevent injuries. Always ensure that your equipment is in good working condition, and check for faults or malfunctions before using it. Exposed power cables can lead to electric shocks, causing short circuits on your equipment, potentially resulting in permanent damage. This can affect your work, and you will be forced to replace any damaged tools.
Some people simply ignore instructions when operating machinery, and this is very dangerous. Different types of equipment come with manufacturer's instructions which should never be undermined. Regardless of your experience in woodworking, it's essential to follow instructions so that you do not end up hurting yourself and regretting silly oversights.

Operating in a Rush

In woodworking, you should be calm, collected, and advance in your work stage by stage to eliminate the chances of making dumb mistakes. If you're working in a rush, you can only realize that you have made a terrible mistake when it's too late, and that nothing can be done about it. When working with delicate wood, it certainly pays off to be patient so that you can achieve the best results.

Inaccurate Measurements

Accuracy is a virtue in woodwork, since different structures consist of pieces with varying measurements. Therefore, when you're designing any structure, make sure you get accurate measurements so that the different pieces perfectly fit. In general, it's better to have additional length than to cut a shorter piece. The advantage of having extra length is that you can reduce it to suit the desired measurement, should the need arise. Measuring from the wrong direction is another foolish mistake that can affect your work negatively. If the piece requires you to measure from the center or along the sides, you should just do it that way, even if it takes more time.

There is nothing more embarrassing as measuring doors that don't fit. If you cut a length that is short by just half an inch, then you're in trouble. In some cases, the pencil line may be too thin, such that it would be hardly visible when cutting your wood. This can lead to wrong or imprecise cuts that impact the right side of the panel. As such, it's essential to maintain accuracy at all levels if you want to achieve a perfect job.

Another dumb mistake that can be costly is getting overconfident when going about your project. Guesswork isn't an option in carpentry, even if you have several years of experience in the field. The other issue is that you may be tempted to change the measurement of a particular piece midway, but fail to account for that change for other pieces in the same structure. It's important to plan your work first to avoid making unnecessary changes that can compromise your project as a whole.

Drips and Runs in the Finish

After carefully designing your structure, it's no time for celebration yet until you put all the finishing touches. Poor painting can compromise the quality of your structure. For example, drips and runs can ruin your project when you're nearly done. Depending on the type of wood used, it's recommended to use a compressor when applying varnish, stain, or paint, to avoid runs that may be difficult to remove without scratching or damaging the wood. The other dumb mistake pertains to polishing and sanding your final product. Failing to use the right grain of sandpaper or sanding equipment can affect the look, feel, and overall quality of your product.

Not Investing in Right Equipment

Another common error most people do in woodworking is not investing in the right tools. Some people purchase cheap tools thinking they will get good results, just like using the right tool for a particular purpose. For instance, cheap wood tends to break easily, so you should get the right supplies for cutting and designing. Know that cheaper tools usually means poorer build, and it can ruin the quality of your work. Low end tools can also break if you forcibly use them on the hardwood; when that happens repeatedly, you'll be forced to procure another tool, which can be costly in the long run. To avoid downtime in your work, consider getting proper equipment in the first place. Even if it costs you some, it's an investment that will pay for itself.

In contrast, some people are tempted to buy sophisticated tools before they even know how to use the ones they already have. If you deal with smaller projects, it's advisable to get the right equipment to avoid wasting money on something that will rarely be used. Furthermore, others may also try to use power tools every time, even when hand tools are more appropriate. Before buying woodworking tools, consult with professionals in the carpentry field so that you know exactly what you want, and why you need it. Getting advice from the wrong person can also be a fatal mistake, which will end up affecting the quality of your work.

To avoid common frustrations, it's imperative that you work on something that you're capable of doing and seeing through. In other words, avoid jumping to bigger projects while you're still a learner. As a matter of fact, you're more likely to get discouraged quickly if you try something complicated instead of focusing on basic and manageable tasks. It's also a good idea to learn from other experienced carpenters and woodworkers to master the technique of accomplishing certain tasks flawlessly.

Ruin a Critical Piece

Some pieces in carpentry are critical and they require sophisticated designs. You can ruin a critical piece by drilling holes that are either too small, or too large. The worst part about certain mistakes is that they're irreversible, and you'd be forced to discard the entire piece. Just imagine the cost of buying the same material again for the same project. So, before you start drilling holes on the board, make sure you're doing it correctly to avoid frustrations over something that could have been avoided with basic logic and reasoning.

Poor Jointing

The other common silly mistake often made by many woodworkers involves the use of wrong jointing when building a structure. There are different types of joints in woodwork, and you must use the right one for a particular purpose. Generally, there are no viable substitutes for that step. When making cabinets, for example, you should use the right joints for the drawers to make them strong. Joints with large gaps and poor fits can compromise your final product.

Wood glue is another essential component in woodworking that shouldn't be overlooked. Even if you're applying nails or screws onto certain joints, you should first apply the glue to make the structure firm and have it sealed properly. Likewise, be careful to avoid improper mixing of adhesive glue that will never dry. The joints will remain loose, and the piece of furniture can easily crumble as a result.

Buying Insufficient Raw Material

A lot of enthusiasts often make the poor decision of not purchasing enough raw materials for a specific project. If you want to produce quality work, then you should buy the right materials and in sufficient quantity, plain and simple. The problem with not getting enough wood is that you'll struggle to match the color and grain when buying additional materials after experiencing shortages. In contrast, the other pitfall that you can avoid pertains to over-buying raw materials for a project. In doing so, you may end up with too much wood that just won't suffice for another building project. This would be a waste if you cannot use the wood elsewhere.

There is also the risk of buying the wrong kind of materials or supplies. For instance, you'll only realize that the fasteners are too long after you've finished your work. Therefore, when buying raw materials, make sure you use the right bill of quantities to avoid misfits and experiencing unnecessary challenges throughout your project.

Running Many Projects Simultaneously

Finally, if you find yourself running more than five projects at the same time in the same workshop, know that you may be heading for disaster. Woodworking requires concentration, and you should take your time to perfect a certain project before moving on to the next one. There is a high chance of not meeting the standard expectations if you work on several tasks simultaneously. The main reason for this is that you'd be forcing yourself to work under pressure, and fail to work diligently. You may also be unable to meet your deadlines for each project.

Some people are just so overly eager that they'll grab every project that comes their way. As a professional, you can end up losing credibility if your customers begin to associate your products with sketchy construction and poor workmanship. At the end of the day, you'll lose clients, which will affect your business in negative ways. In short, you need to be realistic when dealing with customers to gain their trust, instead of prioritizing your quest for quick profits. Give them an honest estimate of the time you expect to finish their work. If you think you won't be able to meet the deadline, it's best to inform them in advance rather than constantly postponing delivery dates or keeping them in the dark. When you're in the business of woodworking, you should ensure that you aim to produce the best quality products that will satisfy the needs of your customers. While mistakes are certainly common, you should do your best to avoid them wherever and whenever possible. However, there are certain dumb woodworking mistakes that can ruin your project if you're not careful and meticulous enough. Such oversights are often caused by an excess of confidence and taking things for granted, which you'll come to regret later. Dumb mistakes can also be costly, and when the mistake is serious and irreversible, you may be forced to abandon the entire project, which is bad news. So, as you progress in this craft, use the times where you fell short as a lesson for the future. Other dumb woodworking errors can lead to injuries, affect your quality and pace of work tremendously. For instance, failing to comply with basic safety precautions while operating power tools can be dangerous, and you'll only regret it when footing medical bills and being forced to suspend your operations. The good news is that these mistakes can be avoided if you take your time in your work, and make that a habit. As we've seen, rushing to complete a project can be a big blunder that should be avoided at all costs. To maintain the quality and consistency of your work, you must always exhibit perseverance and stay razor-focused.

Wrong part placement

During assembly you could find out you got one of the parts placed wrong: this could be on the wrong side or even the wrong face of the board is showing. This can be fixed by marking your pieces while you make them. Having one particular mark for all inside faces will make it possible to find errors at a glance.

Large hole not big enough

You bore a large hole that is too small. Enlarging it is difficult as you can't find the center of the hole anymore. The solution is to put a square plug in the hole. The center of the plug can easily be found so that you can cut your new hole.

Conclusion

You've hopefully learned that woodworking isn't as simple or as hard as some people might deem it to be. The main factors that will determine whether you'll enjoy creating pieces of wooden art are your passion and drive. No matter how many techniques you know or how many tools you have, you won't really be doing woodworking properly if you don't put your heart and vision to it.

There is no shame in not being as good as you thought in the beginning; there's always room for improvement and development, regardless of how experienced you are. Capturing the true essence of wood types into a lively masterpiece requires regular and thorough practice. This book is still intended as a guide to help you navigate the right setup and proper approach to learning the art and craft of woodworking.

Whether you're trying to broaden your woodworking portfolio or learn it from scratch, you should never give up too quickly when learning something new. Use the beginner projects to your advantage to help you learn the ropes without risking anything at all. The more projects you take on, the more flexible you can be with your designs to match whatever idea you initially had in mind.

As your hands start getting used to woodworking, you'll achieve more focus and develop your ability to paint a clear mental picture of the final product. Also, you're bound to notice the gradual formation of your own style as you progress. The development of technology has changed the needs and demands of the market, making woodwork more sophisticated and elaborate than ever before. Nevertheless, this doesn't mean that you don't get to experiment with woodworking in any way you want.

As you let go of the initial reluctance associated with practicing woodworking, you'll learn that there is no standard way to create a great wooden creation, but rather, a combination of your imagination, deftness, and past experience. Of course, you don't have to follow every single tip mentioned in this book to become a great woodworker; so, focus on learning from your mistakes as much as possible.

Thank you, and best of luck on your future woodworking endeavors!

www.ingramcontent.com/pod-product-compliance
Lightning Source LLC
Chambersburg PA
CBHW081628100526
44590CB00021B/3654